Bulimia Nervosa: The Secret Cycle of Bingeing and Purging

Bulimia Nervosa:

The Secret Cycle of Bingeing and Purging

Liza N. Burby

The Rosen Publishing Group/New York

The Teen Health Library of Eating Disorder Prevention

To my daughters, Danielle and Laura, may you never know the pain of an eating disorder, and to my husband, Steve, for all his support.

Acknowledgments:
Special thanks to Dr. Ira Sacker, founder and director of Helping to End Eating Disorders (HEED) at Brookdale University Hospital, for his insight and expertise with this manuscript.

The people pictured in this book are only models. They in no way practice or endorse the activities illustrated. Captions serve only to explain the subjects of photographs and do not in any way imply a connection between the real-life models and the staged situations. News agency photos are exceptions.

Published in 1998 by the Rosen Publishing Group, Inc.
29 East 21st Street, New York, NY 10010

Library of Congress Cataloging-in-Publication Data

Burby, Liza N.
Bulimia nervosa: the secret cycle of bingeing and purging / by Liza Burby.
    p.cm. — (The teen health library of eating disorder prevention)
    Includes bibliographical references and index.
    Summary: Introduces the eating disorder known as bulimia nervosa, including its development, its prevention, and sources of help.
    ISBN 0-8239-2762-8
    1. Bulimia—Juvenile literature. [1. Bulimia. 2. Eating disorders.] I. Title. II. Series.
RC552.B84B88 1998
616.85'263—dc21   98-16888
                                               CIP
                                               AC

Manufactured in the United States of America

Contents

Introduction: The Hidden Disease

"Some days I ate no more than a cup of chicken broth. Other days I felt so out of control about my eating that I couldn't stop. I'd eat a whole bakery cake, a pound of cheese with crackers, and a loaf of bread with butter and jelly. Then I'd wash it down with a 64-ounce bottle of diet soda. When I was done, I felt so nauseous that it was easy to make myself throw up. Then I'd feel drained but relieved that all those calories I had just eaten wouldn't be able to make me fatter. I kept this a secret for years. Not even my family figured out what I was doing."

This young woman struggled with a serious eating disorder known as bulimia nervosa. It is estimated that more than 8 million people in the United States suffer from eating disorders. More than 90 percent of them are female. Recent research shows that 1 in about 400 males between the ages of thirteen and thirty has an eating disorder.

Eating disorders include anorexia nervosa, bulimia nervosa, and binge eating disorder (also known as compulsive eating). Compulsive exercise is also a

Understanding the importance of good nutrition is one way to prevent the onset of eating disorders. The body needs the proper nutrients to grow and function properly.

growing problem. It is identified as a related eating disorder problem by health professionals and eating disorder experts. There are certain characteristics to each disorder, but they all present very dangerous health risks to a person's mind and body.

The reasons why a person develops an eating disorder are complex. They involve people's eating habits, their attitudes about weight and food, their attitudes about body shape, and psychological factors, especially those surrounding the need for control.

Bulimia has been understood only as recently as the 1980s. Although it was first diagnosed in the 1950s, many mental health professionals at that time had not even heard of the problem. Since then, we have learned of famous people who suffered from it, including the late Princess Diana, actresses Ally Sheedy and Jane Fonda, Olympic gymnast Cathy Rigby, tennis champion Zena Garrison, and singer Karen Carpenter.

Today bulimia is a major social concern. It can have devastating effects on the mind and body. Many people are studying the disease and its causes. Many eating disorder experts believe that images in the media put a lot of pressure on young men and women to reach an "ideal" body shape—one that is impossible for most people to achieve.

Now parents, doctors, and school counselors are learning about the early warning signs of bulimia and other eating disorders in young people. Researchers are working to help people recover, but they also understand that more needs to be done to help prevent these harmful disorders in the first place.

This book aims to help you, the reader, protect yourself against the dangers of an eating disorder. Not only will you learn about the effects of bulimia and what to do if you or someone you know is suffering, but you will find ways to improve your self-esteem. And self-esteem is one of the most important things you need to win the fight against eating disorders.

What Is Bulimia?

1

Bulimia nervosa is characterized by the cycle of bingeing and purging. Bingeing is when a person eats a large amount of food in a short period of time. Purging means to rid the body of all the food in order to prevent weight gain. This is done by vomiting or using drugs, such as diuretics or laxatives. Sometimes excessive exercise is also used in an attempt to get rid of the extra calories. Both bingeing and purging are intense, overwhelming urges that become uncontrollable.

It is difficult to say exactly how many people suffer from bulimia because doctors are not required to report it. In addition, many who suffer from bulimia do not seek help. Some studies say that bulimia currently affects 1 to 3 percent of middle and high school girls and 1 to 4 percent of college women. Recent studies also indicate that bulimia is on the rise for males, particularly for men between the ages of twenty-one and twenty-four who are involved in sports and activities that connect weight with performance. Weight lifters, bodybuilders, gymnasts, wrestlers, and jockeys are all at a higher risk for eating disorders. While most people who suffer from bulimia are in their late teens and early twenties, the disorder is affecting people at younger ages than ever before.

Warning Signs of Bulimia

Eating Disorders Awareness and Prevention, Inc. (EDAP) has outlined specific warning signs that indicate a person has bulimia. People with bulimia:

- Believe that they would be happier and more successful if they were thinner
- Have severe mood swings
- Overeat in response to stress or other uncomfortable feelings

- Alternate between strict dieting and overeating
- Show evidence of binge eating, such as buying or stealing large amounts of food. Binge eating means eating a lot of calories—as many as 5,000 or more in one binge. What is considered to be a binge can vary, though. People with bulimia often feel the need to purge after eating small amounts of food as well. The frequency of a binge can also vary from once a month to twenty times a day or more
- Buy certain products, such as syrup of ipecac (used to induce vomiting); have cuts or marks on their knuckles and fingertips from using their fingers to induce vomiting
- Indulge in other types of impulsive behavior, such as abusing drugs, going on shopping sprees, and/or shoplifting

It can be difficult to tell if a person is suffering from an eating disorder. It is especially difficult to diagnose bulimia because the problem is often hidden. Unfortunately, many people struggle with their relationship to food. The behavior of a person in the early stages of bulimia (or another eating disorder)

Sports such as gymnastics demand a certain body type. Some athletes may go to extremes to keep their weight down. They may abuse diet pills and laxatives or make themselves throw up to please a demanding coach.

may not seem out of the ordinary in our culture. This is because we are taught to feel anxious and guilty around food, worry about our weight, and to fear fat. But these warning signs are important to recognize in order to help people. An eating disorder left untreated can be life threatening.

Is Anorexia Different from Bulimia?

Anorexia nervosa is characterized by a refusal to eat

People with bulimia have a distorted body image. No matter what their size, they see themselves as much larger than they really are.

and maintain a healthy body weight. A person who suffers from anorexia nervosa shares symptoms with a person who has bulimia nervosa. This is the reason why "nervosa" is part of both terms. In fact, about 50 percent of people who have bulimia had anorexia first. In both cases, the person is preoccupied with dieting, food, weight, and body size.

But there are also a few differences. People with anorexia deny to themselves and to others that there is a problem. But people with bulimia are aware that there is a problem, even though they may try to keep it a secret from others.

People with anorexia are 15 percent below the recommended weight for their size. Those with bulimia are usually of average weight, though they may weigh ten or fifteen pounds above or below this weight.

But ultimately, the two disorders have more similarities than differences. No matter what they actually weigh, people with bulimia and anorexia always fear that they will get fat—no matter how thin they are. They feel that being thin means being happy. People with anorexia and bulimia have an inability to deal with uncomfortable feelings. They have a distorted body image, seeing their bodies as being much larger than they really are. As a result, they use dangerous methods to lose weight and refuse to eat in a healthy manner.

When a person suffers from bulimia, it is a sign that there is a larger problem in that person's life. When someone can't express how he or she feels, bingeing and purging become the emotional release.

Hannah was fifteen when her father lost his job. At first she believed her parents when they told her that they would be able to manage until her father got a new job. But after a month went by and her father was still unemployed, she became very anxious. She was also having trouble in school. Hannah was the only one of her friends who didn't have a boyfriend. No one had time to hang out with her anymore. Often she ate lunch by herself. As miserable as she was, she did not want to worry her parents, so she kept her feelings to herself.

Hannah started snacking a lot. She bought candy and chips on the way home from school. When she got home, she raided the kitchen cabinets for something to eat. She didn't really know what she wanted. She just knew that there was an uneasy feeling in the pit of her stomach and she wanted it to go away. She would take whole boxes of food up to her room and eat as quickly as possible. She was afraid her parents would find out.

Her parents were too preoccupied at first to notice. So that her parents wouldn't worry, Hannah ate with them each night even though she was full. By the time she was done forcing herself to eat dinner, she usually felt sick. After she helped with the dishes, she would run to the bathroom to make herself throw up. When she was done, she usually felt numb and depressed.

Several months later, Hannah's father was working again. Hannah thought she should feel better, but she couldn't stop herself from bingeing and purging.

No one is immune from the dangers of eating disorders. They affect people of all ages from all walks of life.

Hannah became addicted to her behavior. Once she started bingeing and purging, she found the behavior hard to stop. For Hannah, bingeing was a way to relieve tension. But immediately after her binge, she would feel incredibly anxious about gaining weight. The only way to feel better was to purge. Purging was a way for her to try to regain self-control and get rid of all the negative feelings she had.

When people purge, they are not just getting rid of food. They are also trying to get rid of unwanted feelings like anxiety, anger, guilt, panic, and stress. And it doesn't take very long for the bingeing and purging habit to become an addictive pattern. Although scientists are still researching this idea, some believe the purging may affect chemicals in the brain, causing the person to feel satisfied after an episode. The cycle is repeated to feel this rush after purging. There is a strong need to experience that feeling again. People with bulimia believe that purging is the only way to get those feelings again.

Who's at Risk?

Anyone can develop an eating disorder. While it affects mostly white, middle- to upper-class females, it can happen to males and females of all races, classes, and ages. It can happen to good students who are popular and successful adults who hold good jobs. But it also can happen to people who have problems, such as addiction to drugs or alcohol, as well as people who have been sexually abused or suffer from depression.

Athletes are also vulnerable to eating disorders, particularly with sports that connect weight with performance. It can be a problem for dancers, weight lifters, wrestlers, gymnasts, swimmers, and long-distance runners. Males with eating disorders may be reluctant to get help. They may feel that an eating disorder is a "female problem" and be too embarrassed to seek help.

Eating Is an Emotional Experience

Bulimia turns the act of eating into a self-destructive behavior. Eating is not a pleasurable experience anymore. Food is not just fuel for your body. It is used to deal with uncomfortable feelings: fear, anger, and guilt. A person with bulimia is unable to stop the secret cycle of bingeing and purging because he or she relies upon this ritual to handle those feelings. Soon it has taken over his or her life.

"I stopped eating around other people. I was afraid to go places where I knew there would be food because I couldn't trust myself around it."

"I spent all my time thinking about what to eat, when and where to eat, how to eat without getting caught, when and where I would purge, and how I was going to do it."

Everyone overeats at some point or another. We have all eaten too much on certain occasions or during the holidays, and that's normal. The difference is that someone with bulimia will do it on a regular basis and cannot control the urge to binge. There are many reasons why someone can develop bulimia. The next chapter will discuss certain triggers that may lead someone to develop bulimia nervosa.

Why Do People Develop Bulimia?

2

Bulimia, as well as other eating disorders, tends to be triggered by family and relationship problems. It can start as a result of a comment about your weight from a parent, a friend, or if you're an athlete, from a coach. Bulimia can also be a symptom of a larger problem, such as depression, low self-esteem, or sexual abuse.

Bulimia usually develops at a time in a person's life when a big change is taking place. This could be your parents' divorce, moving to another town, changing schools, or going off to college. It could also be a trauma, such as rape or sexual assault. When these experiences occur during the teen years, when teens are experiencing changes in their bodies, an eating disorder could develop.

Not everyone who has problems in his or her life develops bulimia, but there are ingredients that will make some people more vulnerable to it. One of the main issues that eating disorder experts agree on is the negative influence magazines, advertising, and television have on people's body image. Constant images of perfect models can have harmful effects on a person's self-esteem.

Media Influences

The problem is that movies, television, and all forms of advertising make us feel that there is an ideal way our bodies should look in order to be worthy and acceptable to others. Everywhere we look, from billboards to TV ads, there is pressure to diet and be thin. Americans spend billions of dollars each year on dieting, from weight-loss centers to diet pills and diet books. Advertisers constantly try to convince us, with ads for everything from diet sodas to bathing suits, that if you eat, you'll get fat.

And for many people, there is nothing worse than being fat. One survey by Eating Disorders

Awareness and Prevention, Inc. (EDAP) in Seattle reported that young girls are more afraid of becoming fat than they are of cancer, nuclear war, or losing their parents.

The media sends strong messages to females that they are fat no matter what size they happen to be. As a result, many females, and an increasing number of males, have a distorted body image. They think they need to lose weight, when in fact, they are very healthy at their current body size.

When Katy was fourteen, some schoolmates teased her about her weight in gym class. For the first time, she thought she was fat.

Katy's parents weren't home very often. When Katy started to diet, no one noticed her changing eating habits. She thought the best way to lose weight would be to eat very little. She taped a picture of a thin model to the door of her room and put her scale next to the door. Then she started a diet diary in which she recorded the number of calories she ate each day and how much she weighed each morning.

She lost five pounds in the first week. After that the weight loss slowed. So she figured if she ate even less, she would lose more weight. But soon she started to fantasize about all the foods she wouldn't let herself have.

One day after school, Katy couldn't hold back anymore. She had not done very well on a test that she had felt she was prepared for. She was very upset with herself. She opened the freezer and took out a whole cake. Once she started eating, she found she couldn't stop. She ate the whole thing in one sitting. Afterward she felt horrified and sick to her stomach. Frantically, she exercised in her room that night, desperate to burn all the calories she had consumed.

A pattern began to develop. Every day Katy would weigh herself and record her caloric intake. She could go for a few days at a time on her strict diet. Then something would happen in school or at home that would send her into a binge. Katy eventually turned to a combination of laxatives and exercise to help purge.

Katy knew she had a problem and she was miserable, but she didn't know how to stop it. She was angry with herself, but too ashamed to talk about it with her family and friends.

Dieting

What happens when people feel that they're not good enough because they're not thin enough? They usually think a diet is the answer to all their problems. But diets are dangerous because they set up an unhealthy relationship with food. In fact, while not all diets lead to eating disorders, 80 percent of all eating disorders started with a diet.

Diets are not healthy. When people restrict their food intake, they are depriving themselves. This can cause people to become obsessed with everything they feel they are missing. It is natural for the body to rebel against the diet.

When your body is deprived of food, it reacts as if it were being attacked. Your metabolism slows down, and your body burns fewer calories. This is because your body is trying to hold on to the little food it's getting. The body reacts to dieting by storing fat more efficiently to survive.

When people break their diets, it often results in a binge. Breaking a diet can cause feelings of guilt. The only way to relieve that guilt is to purge.

Family Issues

Sometimes, parents who are concerned about their own weight cause their children to worry about their weight, too.

"My mom started to comment on everything I ate about the same time I started puberty. 'You'll get fat if you eat that,' she told me every time I reached for a snack. When my body started to fill out a year later, I was already dieting and on my way to developing an unhealthy relationship with food. Nobody told me that gaining weight is a normal process during puberty."

Food is also an important part of our family rituals, from Thanksgiving dinner to birthday cake to

Children learn at a very young age that social occasions often revolve around food. For many cultures around the world, food bonds the family together.

everyday meals. Research has shown that young children will eat according to their physical hunger. They naturally regulate their food intake. This means they will refuse even one more bite of food if they are full. But parents soon interfere with their children's eating patterns. Parents take control over what their children eat around the time children turn three and four. When this happens, children learn to eat for reasons other than hunger.

Food takes on a different meaning. For example, you learn at a very young age what is okay to eat after school or what is not allowed before dinner. You may be told that candy and other sweets are "bad" for you, but you are given such foods as

It's important for people suffering from depression to seek professional help to learn how to deal with painful and uncomfortable feelings in a healthy way.

rewards for "good" behavior such as fair play or achievement in school.

Sometimes there are other, more serious problems in families that can contribute to the onset of bulimia or other eating disorders. People may be at risk if they come from homes in which someone suffers from depression, a parent has an alcohol or drug abuse problem, or a parent is physically and/or sexually abusive.

Depression

Depression is a psychological disorder marked by extreme sadness, inactivity, isolation, extreme fatigue, difficulty in concentrating, increased or decreased appetite, sleep disturbances, feelings of hopelessness, and sometimes suicidal tendencies. People who suffer from depression often develop bulimia. Experts are studying the link between eating disorders and depression.

Depression is genetic, which means it runs in families. Bulimia may also be linked to genetics. This means if a family member suffers from depression and/or an eating disorder, you may be at a higher risk for developing one or both of these disorders. No one knows for sure how much of a person's eating disorder is caused by chemical or biological factors. This is the least understood cause of eating disorders, but more is being discovered every day.

Drug Abuse

In a home in which a parent is an alcoholic or drug abuser, children live in an almost constant state of

In a dysfunctional family environment, children are unable to rely on their parents for love and support and must take on more than their share of family responsibilities.

disorder and dysfunction. You may never know from one minute to the next how your parent will act. You may be afraid to have friends visit. You may spend lots of time alone taking care of yourself. An eating disorder may be a cry for help in this lonely situation, or it may be a way to take control of some part of your life— over what you eat, how much you eat, and when, and even how you can rid your body of food.

Jack is eighteen years old. He gets straight As, he's president of the student council, and he recently won the state championship in track and field. He's also preparing for college in the fall.

Jack should be enjoying his senior year, but life at home is so chaotic that he sometimes feels he leads two different lives. Jack's mother is an alcoholic. Every day when he comes home from school, he doesn't know if he will find her drunk at the kitchen table or up in her studio working on her paintings.

When she is working, he doesn't mind being home. But on days when she has been drinking, he can't seem to get away from her. She follows him through the house and it is hard for him to get his schoolwork done. When his father gets home from work, his parents immediately start fighting.

Lately, Jack is trying not to come home at all. He stays after school to run around the track, each day trying to beat his record from the day before.

Some people use exercise to purge calories from their systems. This is often referred to as exercise bulimia.

Sometimes he's so exhausted that he can barely move. When he finally has to go home, he sneaks up to his room and hides out there.

Since there are no family meals anymore, he usually buys lots of junk food on his way home. While he does his homework, he binges. Usually after eating like this, Jack feels disgusted with himself. To get rid of all the *calories, he goes running again. Sometimes, he also abuses laxatives.*

Jack is often lightheaded and finds it harder and harder to work up the energy to run. After each binge-and-purge episode, Jack promises himself he'll never do it again. But the next day, he always breaks his promise.

Problems like Jack's don't suddenly develop when a person is a teenager or young adult. In most cases, the family's problems have been going on for a long time. Research shows that the behavior that triggers bulimia begins in childhood. In fact, studies indicate that girls in particular become anxious about food and their weight as young as age five or six. This behavior can set children up for a lifelong battle with their body image and could lead to bulimia or another eating disorder.

Physical and Sexual Abuse

Some children are abused physically, verbally, or sexually by a parent, a friend, a relative, or another trusted adult. The betrayal and pain they experience can lead to severe emotional problems. The eating disorder can be a way to bury those painful feelings and ease the emotional pain. People who are sexually abused grow up with little or no sense of control over their own bodies. Bulimia is an attempt to regain control.

It may also be a way for people to punish themselves because they feel they don't deserve to be happy. When people don't feel worthy enough to express what they want, it can manifest itself by bingeing and purging behavior. Bingeing represents the overwhelming desires, and purging represents the punishment for trying to fulfill those desires.

No Easy Answers

An eating disorder like bulimia is a very complex issue. Just because someone feels out of control about life does not mean that he or she will develop an eating disorder. Often there are many other things happening in a person's life that trigger the problem.

Ultimately there is no one cause of an eating disorder. There are many different factors that contribute to it. The person who is experiencing it usually does not consciously decide to develop an eating disorder. It's an unconscious process. The bottom line is that the eating disorder itself is actually an expression of other problems in a person's life. It may be a way for a person to feel he or she has some control. It may be a way for someone to feel a sense of identity, independence, even security.

Recovering from an eating disorder involves uncovering the causes and learning how to deal with those problems in a healthy way. And the earlier a person deals with those problems, the easier it is to get better.

How Bulimia Affects the Body and Mind

3

Bulimia, like all eating disorders, can have devastating effects on the mind and body. It's important to understand the dangers of this disorder.

Physical Consequences

There are several common medical problems that people with bulimia can develop. If bulimia is left untreated, a person may need to be hospitalized. The longer the eating disorder remains untreated, the worse the problems become.

In females, bulimia can cause an irregular menstrual cycle or even the loss of it, which is called amenorrhea. New studies have found that this can cause other problems, as well. Women who don't get their periods lack enough estrogen, which helps maintain strong bones. A lack of estrogen can cause osteoporosis, a disease that weakens the bones. When the bones are weak, they break easily. For some athletes, this can cause what doctors are calling the female athlete triad.

The Female Athlete Triad

The female athlete triad is named after the three health problems that occur together in many female athletes: disordered eating, loss of menstrual periods, and loss of bone mass. Any one of these conditions can signal that the body's essential nutrients and tissues are being raided, usually by a combination of starvation and overexercising.

When all three conditions appear at the same time, it is a health emergency. Experts say that as many as 30 percent of female athletes in sports such as gymnastics, long-distance running, and figure skating suffer from the female athlete triad.

Some athletes binge and purge because they believe it will make them better players. But bulimia will ultimately hurt their performance and severely damage their bodies.

Sandy is an honor-roll student and is also on her high school softball and basketball teams. She has been involved in sports since she was in kindergarten. But when she was in the ninth grade, she became uncomfortable about wearing the tight softball uniforms. She thought she looked fat. One day after softball practice, one of her teammates told her about purging. She told Sandy she could eat whatever she wanted and not gain any weight. Shortly after that, Sandy forced herself to vomit.

Her parents found out about it right away. This made Sandy feel guilty and ashamed. But she just became more secretive about bingeing and purging. She *continued to do it, as much as five times a day. She tried laxatives, too. She had frequent dizzy spells, her eyes were bloodshot from vomiting, and her hands had sores on them from forcing herself to vomit.*

Vitamin and Mineral Deficiencies

Dehydration from purging causes dry skin, brittle nails and hair, loss of hair, or bleeding gums from the lack of vitamins and minerals in the body. Purging rituals also take food out of the body before its nutrients can be absorbed. Without these nutrients, the body is at risk for malnutrition even if that person is not too thin and eats regular meals at other times.

The pressure of repeated vomiting can cause the blood vessels in the face, legs, and arms to break, causing little red lines in the skin. Purging can also cause puffiness and swelling in the hands, feet, or face. Because of enlarged salivary glands, people with bulimia usually have swollen cheeks. In addition to fatigue, skin problems, and weak eyesight, vitamin and mineral deficiencies can also cause serious harm to the person's heart, kidneys, and bones.

The teeth develop cavities or raggedy edges, and the gums may be swollen and tender. This happens because repeated vomiting brings stomach acids into the mouth. These acids, strong enough to break down foods, are also strong enough to wear away tooth enamel and the softer tissues of the mouth. If a person vomits frequently, he or she is likely to develop tooth decay and gum disease, and possibly lose many teeth.

Stomach and Organ Damage

Vomiting is a violent reflex that batters the esophagus and stomach lining. The damage is invisible, but so serious that it can be painful for a person to swallow anything, even water. Over time, a person's body will have trouble keeping any food down. The body will purge as an automatic reflex to eating. In severe cases, erosion of the esophagus and/or stomach lining develops. A hole in the esophagus can cause sudden death.

A person with bulimia will also have severe stomach pains. A person may also have frequent cramps and indigestion. Vomiting and laxative abuse can cause painful intestinal spasms. If someone purges frequently with laxatives, he or she may become constipated and become dependent on laxatives for normal bowel movements.

When a person fasts, the body sees it as an emergency. If the fast continues for several days, the body will use the fat deposits and then muscle. The body will then take nutrients from organs, such as the liver and heart.

The most serious side effect of bulimia is an electrolyte imbalance. Repeated purging causes a depletion

Constant vomiting can result in severe cramping and eventually lead to an ulcer, or hole, in the stomach lining.

of the electrolytes potassium, chlorine, and sodium. These are electrically charged ions necessary for all of the body's major systems to function. Athletes drink electrolyte replacements such as Gatorade when they are using a lot of energy in competition. Electrolyte imbalance can cause kidney problems, muscle spasms, heart irregularities, and even death.

Medications such as ipecac are especially dangerous. Parents use ipecac in an emergency to make their children vomit if they accidentally swallow poison. If it isn't used properly, it, too, can be a poison. It will stay in your cells for the rest of your life. If you take it regularly for even a few weeks, you can die. People who have overused it have died from congestive heart failure.

Emotional Problems

When all of a person's time and energy is focused on weight and what he or she is or isn't eating, it can take a big emotional toll on someone's life. People suffering from bulimia often feel guilty and ashamed. The intense feelings of anxiety and tension that accompany the bingeing and purging may be overwhelming. There is also fear when people realize they are hurting their bodies. Most frightening of all is the belief that there is no way to make it all stop.

"I felt so out of control during a binge. I would totally zone out. I didn't even taste any of the food I was shoveling into my body. I ate and ate until I was in so much pain, I had to throw it all up. I couldn't remember what it felt like to be truly hungry."

"I had no energy to go to class or even to hang out with my friends. I felt so alone. I would stay home all the time, feeling depressed. I knew no one wanted to be around me. I was obsessed. The worse I felt, the more I binged. Nothing made sense anymore. The only thing I knew was I had to purge. I had no choice."

A person with bulimia also becomes very protective of his or her rituals. There is usually strong resistance to getting help because it means giving up the behavior that initially gives feelings of control. People with bulimia usually believe they are in control although they get more and more out of control as the disease progresses. A person's self-image becomes increasingly distorted because he or she often has little contact with other people. These feelings can be devastating. In the worst cases, a person may consider suicide as the only way out.

If you think you may suffer from an eating disorder, it's extremely important to get professional help. It's also important to remember that you are not alone and help is available. Consider speaking with someone you trust, such as a parent, a friend, or a counselor. You can also contact one of the organizations listed at the end of this book for more information and help. Recovery is a long process, but with help, many people do get better. In the end, recovery will save your life.

Recovering from Bulimia

4

Jamal was a sophomore in high school when his parents divorced. That year he heard some friends talking about another guy who made himself throw up after meals. Jamal had never been happy with his body. Sometimes even his friends teased him about it. One night after dinner, he tried making himself throw up. Soon, he started eating a big lunch in school. Then, before his next class, he'd go to the bathroom to vomit. He thought he had discovered a great way to eat whatever he wanted. Over time, he was making himself vomit five to six times a day. He never did it *again at home, though, because he didn't want his mother to hear. Dinner became the only meal of the day that he kept down, but he tried to eat as little as possible. He always told his mother he wasn't that hungry.*

Jamal had teeth marks on his hands from putting his fingers down his throat to make himself vomit. Eventually his friends became concerned. They tried talking to him. At first Jamal told them he was fine. He was embarrassed about his behavior. But later that week, he called an eating disorder clinic in his area. He spoke confidentially with someone who urged Jamal to get help. He agreed to enroll in a recovery program.

Jamal was lucky his friends tried to help him. Many people who suffer from bulimia are so caught up in the cycle they don't know how or who to ask for help.

Helping a Loved One

You may notice some of the warning signs of an eating disorder in a friend or relative. If you do, speak up. It may not be easy to do. It can feel as if you are betraying a loved one. But the person needs help. Approach your friend gently and tell him or her that you're worried and listen sympathetically.

Try to understand that your friend may not admit there is a problem. If that happens, don't force your friend to get help. Give your friend support. You can give the person a list of places to go for help or people to call, including the school counselor. Even if your friend doesn't want help, he or she may use the list at another time.

If you see your friend is not listening to you, and you feel it is an emergency situation, confide in a trusted friend or family member. Talk to your school nurse or counselor. An emergency situation is if your friend is throwing up blood, has a very severe stomachache, throws up several times a day, or talks of suicide. Your friend may be angry, but you should react immediately because your friend's life is in danger.

You may feel sad or frustrated if your loved one isn't getting help or you feel you didn't do enough to help that person. Talking to an outsider can remind you that you are not responsible for your friend. You can only help your friend to help himself or herself.

Individual Therapy

Experts say there is no one way for a person to recover from bulimia and there are no miracle cures. You may have to try a few different types of treatment before one works. Although some people recover without therapy, the majority need some type of help from others.

Most experts agree any type of eating disorder therapy must have two parts. The first part is to take care of any medical problems patients may have and to teach them to eat in a healthy way. The second part

Talking with a trained counselor is one of the first steps toward recovery.

is to nurture patients' psychological well-being. This means helping them to understand why they developed bulimia in the first place and how they can change their thinking and behavior so that they can prevent it from continuing. Some will also need medications, such as antidepressants, to help them deal with depression and other feelings bulimia can cause.

Treating bulimia can be a long and complicated process. Some have said that recovering from bulimia was the toughest job they've ever had. Once a person is in a treatment program, it may take as long as six months to two years before he or she can stop the binge-purge cycle, but there is no specific time frame for recovery. The longer someone has had bulimia, the harder it is to break the habits. The earlier it is treated, the better chances there are for recovery.

The Chance of Relapse

Often people have many setbacks. Jesse, who had bulimia for two years, was doing well in therapy until her mother got sick. Then Jesse started bingeing and purging again. This lasted for two months before she was able to get back on track again with the help of her therapist. In other words, a person cannot change obsessive behavior overnight and there will be good times and bad times during recovery.

About half of patients with bulimia recover completely. Another quarter will have some problems throughout their lives, and the remainder never fully recover. New research indicates that some people recovering from bulimia will have to worry about relapse in the same way that a person with an addiction to alcohol must deal with relapse. It is a very real part of the recovery process.

When people have a drug or alcohol addiction, the most important part of their treatment is to stop using those chemicals. They can avoid situations where they might be tempted to use them. But those

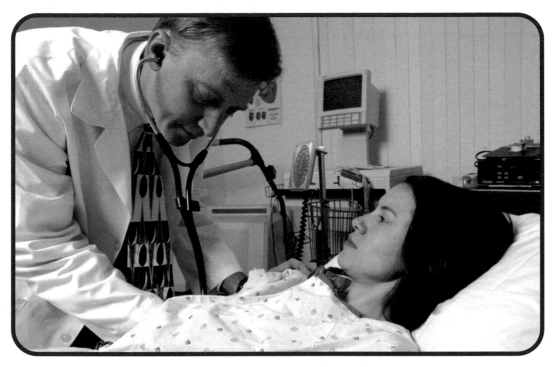

When the symptoms of bulimia become severe, hospitalization is necessary to address possible life-threatening problems. Then therapy to deal with emotional issues can begin.

with bulimia cannot stay away from food. They need to eat. But a treatment program will help them eat in a healthy way. This is not easy.

Hospitalization

If the situation is an emergency, people with bulimia may be hospitalized. This will happen if:

- ❑ Eating behavior is out of control; they are bingeing and purging several times each day and throwing up blood
- ❑ They are suffering from severe depression and/or have thoughts of suicide

- They also have a drug or alcohol dependency
- They are unable to cope with life stresses
- They are suffering from dehydration or an electrolyte imbalance

Family Therapy

Families coping with a member who has an eating disorder often need healing. In order to help improve relationships, the family will go through therapy, too.

For families in which a problem such as abuse contributed to the eating disorder, treatment is even more important. It will not help the person who is in recovery if he or she continues to live with an abusive family. When a family problem, such as divorce or death, cannot be changed, the recovering person must learn new ways to cope.

Group Therapy/Support Groups

Group therapy (also called a support group) is also usually recommended. This is when a person with an eating disorder joins others who have similar experiences to talk about what they've been through and their feelings. It can be a powerful, yet scary process. Knowing you're not the only one with bulimia can help you feel less ashamed. It is also very comforting to be able to talk about your pain with people who will understand because they, too, have lived through it. That's why it is so important for people suffering from bulimia to reach out to others through support groups.

Support groups are an important part of eating disorder treatment, but they are not a substitute for professional counseling. There are many different types of support groups and they are all very effective if the participants are willing to work hard to get well.

According to Anorexia Nervosa and Related Eating Disorders, Inc. (ANRED), 20 percent of people who don't get treatment for eating disorders die. This is why treatment is essential. Those who do get treatment greatly increase their chances of survival and full recovery. If you are suffering from an eating disorder, please consider getting treatment and give yourself the chance to recover.

Developing a Positive Body Image

In this book, we've discussed different causes and triggers that can lead to eating disorders. But there are also many things you can do to prevent them. Many experts believe the sooner you work to change your self-image, the better you will be at handling many of life's challenges and avoiding the possible dangers of eating disorders.

Please consider talking right away to a parent or someone else you trust if you find yourself starting to spend a lot of time thinking or talking about food, your weight, calories, and dieting.

Some other things to watch for are:

- ❑ If you have the need to "burn off" calories with an unreasonable exercise routine; if you exercise despite injury or never feel that you've exercised enough
- ❑ If you are withdrawing from or avoiding activities that make you feel self-conscious about your weight
- ❑ If you are anxious about your weight even after you lose weight

Talk About Your Feelings

If something has changed in your life—your parents recently divorced, a family member is ill, or a good friend moved away—don't hide your feelings. Find someone to talk to about what's on your mind. A school guidance counselor is a good place to start. Some towns have local hotlines for teens to call if they need someone to talk to. Some schools have peer support groups, so you can talk to your classmates about your concerns. The important thing to do is never keep your feelings of distress a secret. Try to talk to your parents or anyone else you trust.

Talking with your friends can be comforting. It will show you that other people have similar feelings and experiences.

Take Care of Your Body

You also need to take care of your body. It's not easy to always eat healthy foods. People eat what's convenient and easy because of busy schedules and busy lives. But it's smart to try and make lifestyle changes.

There are healthier ways to improve your overall health and fitness than the quick fixes offered by fad diets, pills, or bingeing and purging. The problem with fad diets and diet pills is they don't teach you to change your eating habits so that you eat right most of the time. If you have a well-balanced diet that includes proteins, dairy, fruits, vegetables, and grains, your body will be healthy. And that's the most important thing. It's not how much you weigh that matters. It's important to eat right and exercise moderately because it's good for your body and mind.

Many experts are now questioning the importance of weight when it comes to a person's health. There is new research that suggests people who eat right and do moderate exercise are healthy no matter what they weigh. Remember your body shape and size is determined mostly by genetics. You have only so much control over what your body looks like. Look at yourself as an individual with very unique characteristics. Try not to compare yourself to an unrealistic ideal. Also remember you are focusing on learning new and healthy eating habits.

And don't forget to exercise, too. It can be a mile-long walk three times a week, swimming at the local YMCA or YWCA, or exercise classes. The important thing is to focus on all the wonderful things your body can do, not what you think is wrong with it. If you make healthy eating a natural part of your life, you can protect yourself against the dangerous habits that lead to an eating disorder, and you can learn to love your body and the person inside it!

If you're concerned about your weight, talk to your parents or your doctor. The doctor can help you make healthy decisions about your body and explain the positive aspects of a healthy lifestyle.

Playing sports with friends is a fun and healthy way to get your heart rate going. When not taken to extremes, exercise increases self-confidence and makes you eager to take on new challenges.

Preventing Eating Disorders

Even after you've learned why it's important to accept and love your body, it's not an easy thing to do. This is because we live in a culture that rewards the thin and punishes the fat. And these ideas can be reinforced by our families and friends. But that doesn't mean that we have to listen to or believe these harmful messages. You are not powerless against them. There are many ways that you can fight back and make a difference in the prevention of eating disorders for yourself and for others.

Write a Letter

You are a consumer and should feel free to write letters and make phone calls when you see or experience an example of weight discrimination in the media. Don't like what you see in the latest issue of your favorite magazine? Tell them what you think. If you don't see the changes you want, stop buying it. You can send a message to advertisers when you make decisions about what you will and won't buy. If you see something on television that upsets you, write a letter to the network. Network executives do care about what viewers think.

People often find fighting against society's messages helps them change their own beliefs. Fighting back can provide a release for all those negative thoughts.

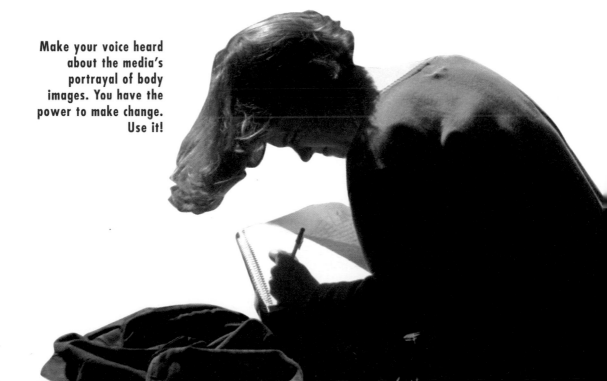

Make your voice heard about the media's portrayal of body images. You have the power to make change. Use it!

Rebel Against Diet Culture

There are activist movements in our country that challenge society's thinking about weight. There are zines, newsletters, magazines, and books promoting the idea that all body shapes are beautiful. These movements are responsible for producing the new fashion magazine *Mode* for women sizes 12 and up and for convincing clothing stores to carry hip clothes in larger sizes.

There are many organizations you can join in the fight against diet culture. EDAP organizes Eating Disorders Awareness Week the first week of February every year. They call the Friday during that week "Fearless Friday." On that day, everyone agrees not to diet but rather to eat in a healthy way. The National Association to Advance Fat Acceptance (NAAFA) also works hard to fight prejudice against obesity. It organizes its own "No Diet Day" on May 5. It is hoped eventually everyone will completely rid their lives of diets.

Stop Negative Talk

It's easy to fall into the trap of talking negatively about yourself. But stop and think about what you are saying. Would you say those things to a friend or a family member? It's important to talk to yourself the way you would to a loved one.

Changing these inner thoughts takes time, but it's important to value yourself for the qualities that matter, such as generosity, sensitivity, intelligence—things that make you a unique individual. The next time you start to put yourself down, say something positive instead. Practice these statements developed by Michael Levine, Ph.D. of EDAP, then share them with your friends:

- ❑ I know being thin does not make me a happier person
- ❑ I won't compare my body with others'
- ❑ I will do things that make me feel good and don't revolve around my body shape and size
- ❑ I will exercise because it's fun and it makes me feel good, not because it burns calories
- ❑ I will eat nutritious foods because they taste good and are good for my health, not because they'll help me lose weight
- ❑ I will value others for who they are, not because of what they look like
- ❑ I will value myself for who I am, not because of what I look like

Remember, the changes you make now will help you keep a positive self-image in the future. Invest in yourself. You are worth it!

Glossary

addiction An obsessive/compulsive need for and use of a substance or behavior.

amenorrhea When a woman who is not pregnant stops getting her period.

antidepressant A drug to relieve or prevent depression.

binge To eat uncontrollably.

calorie A unit for measuring the energy that food supplies to the body.

dehydration The loss of an excessive amount of water or body fluids.

depression A feeling of sadness that lasts a long time and needs to be treated with the help of therapy and/or medication.

diuretic A drug that causes an increase in the amount of urine the kidneys produce.

electrolyte imbalance A serious condition in which a person doesn't have enough of the minerals necessary for healthy body function.

esophagus The tube through which food passes from your throat to your stomach.

estrogen A female hormone.

fasting Going for a period of time without eating any food.

genetic Relating to how people inherit traits and appearances from their parents.

laxative A substance that brings on a bowel movement.

menstrual cycle A monthly cycle including the making of hormones, the thickening of the uterine lining, the shedding of the uterine lining, and menstruation (bleeding).

nutrients Proteins, minerals, and vitamins a person needs to live and grow.

osteoporosis A condition in which the bones become fragile.

psychological Having to do with the mind.

puberty The time when your body becomes sexually mature.

purge To clear the body of food, usually through vomiting, exercise, or laxatives.

relapse A recurrence of symptoms of a disease or condition from which there has been improvement.

Where to Go for Help

American Anorexia/Bulimia Association
165 West 46th Street, Suite 1108
New York, NY, 10036
(212) 575-6200
Web site: http://members.aol.com/AMANBU

Anorexia Nervosa and Related Eating Disorders, Inc. (ANRED)
P.O. Box 5102
Eugene, OR, 97405
(541) 344-1144
Web site: http://www.anred.com.

The Eating Disorder Connection
(900) 737-4044
This is a 24-hour nationwide 900 line that handles calls for referrals, information requests, and crises: (99 cents per minute)

Eating Disorders Awareness and Prevention, Inc. (EDAP)
603 Stewart Street, #803
Seattle, WA 98101
(206) 382-3587
Web site: http://members.aol.com/edapinc

Helping to End Eating Disorders (HEED)
Brookdale University Hospital
9620 Church Avenue
Brooklyn, NY 11212
(718) 240-6451
Web site: http://www.eatingdis.com

National Association of Anorexia Nervosa and Associated Disorders (ANAD)
Box 7
Highland Park, IL 60035
(847) 831-3438
Web site: http://www.members.aol.com/
anad20/index.html

National Eating Disorders Organization (NEDO)
6655 South Yale Avenue
Tulsa, OK 74136
(918) 481-4044
Web site: http://www.laureate.com

In Canada

Anorexia Nervosa and Associated Disorders (ANAD)
109 – 2040 West 12th Avenue
Vancouver, BC V6J 2G2
(604) 739-2070

The National Eating Disorder Information Centre
200 Elizabeth Street
College Wing, 1st Floor, Room 211
Toronto, ON M5G 2C4
(416) 340-4156

Web Sites

The Body Shop
A Web site dedicated to improving the self-esteem and self-respect of all people.
http://www.the-body-shop.com

gURL
An online zine for young women with good straight talk about body image.
http://www.gurl.com

Go, girl! Magazine
An on-line fitness magazine full of positive information and images for young women.
http://www.gogirlmag.com

Something-Fishy Eating Disorders
A helpful Web site that provides information on all aspects of eating disorders.
http://www.something-fishy.com/ed.htm

For Further Reading

Berg, Frances. *Afraid to Eat: Children and Teens in Weight Crisis.* Hettinger, ND: Healthy Weight Publishing Network, 1997.

Bode, Janet. *Food Fight: A Guide to Eating Disorders for Preteens and Their Parents.* New York: Simon and Schuster, 1997.

Cooke, Kaz. *Real Gorgeous: The Truth About Body and Beauty.* New York: W. W. Norton, 1996.

Crook, Marion. *Looking Good: Teenagers and Eating Disorders.* Toronto: NC Press, Ltd., 1992.

Hall, Lindsey, and Leigh Cohn. *Bulimia: A Guide to Recovery.* Carlsbad, CA: Gürze Books, 1986.

Kolodny, Nancy J. *When Food's a Foe: How You Can Confront and Conquer Your Eating Disorder.* New York: Little, Brown and Company, 1992.

Kubersky, Rachel. *Everything You Need to Know About Eating Disorders.* Rev. ed. New York: Rosen Publishing, 1998.

Maloney, Michael, and Rachel Kranz. *Straight Talk About Eating Disorders.* New York: Facts on File, 1991.

Sacker, Ira, M.D., and Marc A. Zimmer, Ph.D. *Dying to Be Thin: Understanding and Defeating Anorexia Nervosa and Bulimia—A Practical, Lifesaving Guide*. New York: Warner Books, 1987.

The following books can be ordered directly from Gürze Books, P.O. Box 2238, Carlsbad, CA 92018-9883; (800) 756-7533. They will be sent in a plain, confidential package.

Cohen, Mary Anne. *French Toast for Breakfast: Declaring Peace with Emotional Eating.*

Hall, Lindsey, ed. *Full Lives: Women Who Have Freed Themselves from Obsession with Food and Weight.*

Zerbe, Kathryn. *The Body Betrayed: A Deeper Understanding of Women, Eating Disorders, and Treatment.*

Index

About the Author

Liza N. Burby is the author of thirty-two other Rosen books, as well as four nonfiction books for young adults. She is a parenting columnist for *Newsday* and a frequent contributor to several national magazines. She has written several articles about bulimia. In addition, she speaks to students and adults about topics such as eating disorders and family violence. She lives in Huntington, New York, with her husband and two young daughters.

Design and Layout: Christine Innamorato

Consulting Editor: Michele I. Drohan

Photo Credits

Photo on p. 7 by John Bentham; pp. 10, 13 © Michael Krasowitz/FPG International; p.14 © Jim Cummins/FPG International; pp. 17, 37 by Ira Fox; p. 20 © Willie Hill/FPG International; pp. 25, 50 © Telegraph Colour Library/FPG International; p. 26 by Seth Dinnerman; p. 27 © Stephanie Rausser/FPG International; p. 29 © Jill Sabella/FPG International; pp. 32, 40 by Les Mills; p. 43 © Dusty Willison/International Stock; p. 48 © James Davis/International Stock; p. 52 by Jim Cummins.